Withdrawn

AMAZING ORIGAMI

Origami
Pets

Lisa Miles

Gareth Stevens
Publishing

Please visit our website, www.garethstevens.com. For a free color catalog of all our high-quality books, call toll free 1-800-542-2595 or fax 1-877-542-2596.

Library of Congress Cataloging-in-Publication Data

Miles, Lisa.
   Origami pets / Lisa Miles.
     pages   cm. – (Amazing origami)
   Includes index.
   ISBN 978-1-4339-9657-3 (pbk.)
   ISBN 978-1-4339-9658-0 (6-pack)
   ISBN 978-1-4339-9656-6 (library binding)
   1. Origami–Juvenile literature. 2. Pets–Juvenile literature.   I. Title.
   TT872.5.M554 2013
   736'.982–dc23

                                                    2012050329

First Edition

Published in 2014 by
Gareth Stevens Publishing
111 East 14th Street, Suite 349
New York, NY 10003

Copyright © 2014 Arcturus Publishing

Models and photography: Belinda Webster and Michael Wiles
Text: Lisa Miles
Design: Emma Randall
Editors: Anna Brett, Becca Clunes, and Joe Harris
Animal photography: Shutterstock

Printed in the United States of America

CPSIA compliance information: Batch #CS13GS: For further information contact Gareth Stevens, New York, New York at 1-800-542-2595.

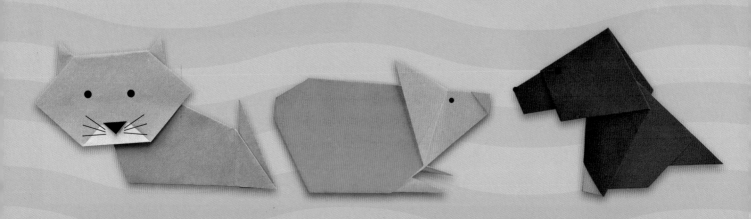

Contents

Basic Folds

Origami has been popular in Japan for hundreds of years and is now loved all around the world. You can make great origami models with just one sheet of paper... and this book shows you how!

The paper used in origami is thin but strong, so that it can be folded many times. It is usually colored on one side. You can also use ordinary scrap paper, but make sure it's not too thick.

Origami models often share the same folds and basic designs, known as "bases." This introduction explains some of the folds and bases that you will need for the projects in this book. When making the models, follow the key below to find out what the lines and arrows mean. And always crease well!

KEY

valley fold   - - - - - - - - - - - - - -

mountain fold   ....

step fold (mountain and valley fold next to each other)

direction to move paper

push

MOUNTAIN FOLD

To make a mountain fold, fold the paper so that the crease is pointing up toward you, like a mountain.

VALLEY FOLD

To make a valley fold, fold the paper the other way, so that the crease is pointing away from you, like a valley.

INSIDE REVERSE FOLD

An inside reverse fold is useful if you want to make a nose or a tail, or if you want to flatten the shape of another part of an origami model.

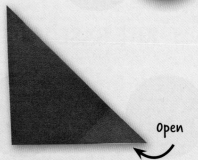

Open

① Practice by first folding a piece of paper diagonally in half. Make a valley fold on one point and crease.

② It's important to make sure that the paper is creased well. Run your finger over the crease two or three times.

③ Unfold and open up the corner slightly. Refold the crease nearest to you into a mountain fold.

④ Open up the paper a little more and then tuck the tip of the point inside. Close the paper. This is the view from the underside of the paper.

⑤ Flatten the paper. You now have an inside reverse fold.

OUTSIDE REVERSE FOLD

An outside reverse fold is useful if you want to make a head, beak, foot, or another part of your model that sticks out.

① Practice by first folding a piece of paper diagonally in half. Make a valley fold on one point and crease.

② It's important to make sure that the paper is creased well. Run your finger over the crease two or three times.

③ Unfold and open up the corner slightly. Refold the crease farthest away from you into a valley fold.

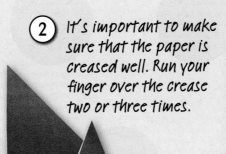

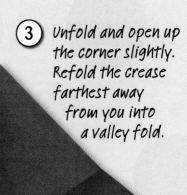

Open

④ Open up the paper a little more and start to turn the corner inside out. Then close the paper when the fold begins to turn.

⑤ You now have an outside reverse fold. You can either flatten the paper or leave it rounded out.

Bases

KITE BASE

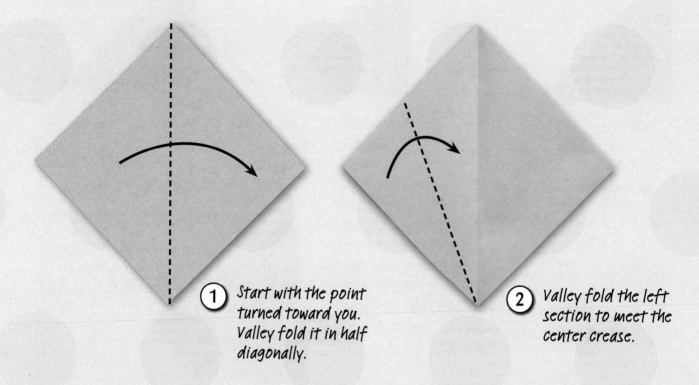

1. Start with the point turned toward you. Valley fold it in half diagonally.

2. Valley fold the left section to meet the center crease.

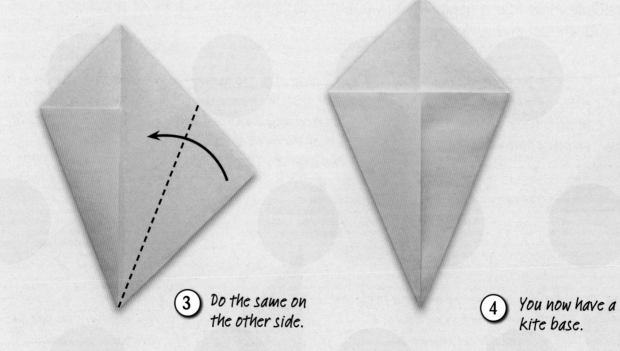

3. Do the same on the other side.

4. You now have a kite base.

FISH BASE

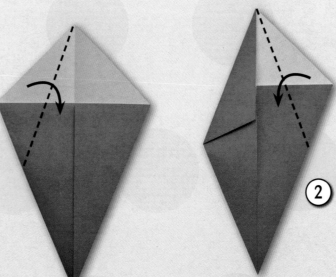

(1) Make a kite base, as shown on page 6. Valley fold the left corner.

(2) Do the same on the other side.

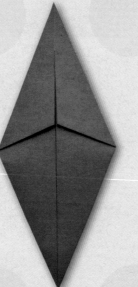

(3) The paper should now look like this.

open

(4) Open out the top left corner. Take hold of the inside flap and pull it down to meet the center crease to make a new flap, as shown.

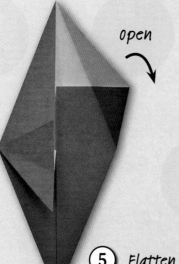

open

(5) Flatten the paper. Then do the same on the other side.

(6) You now have a fish base.

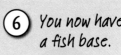

Cat

Cats have lived with people as pets for thousands of years. They make good companions as they are friendly and love to sit on laps!

MAKE THE HEAD

(1) Begin with a square of paper colored side down, and turn the point towards you. Valley fold it in half diagonally.

(2) Open it out, then valley fold the top tip to meet the center crease.

(3) Valley fold the top section down along the center crease.

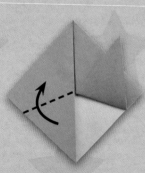

(4) Valley fold the right corner down.

(5) Do the same on the other side.

(6) Valley fold the bottom right corner up.

(7) Do the same on the other side. These are the cat's ears.

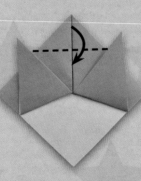

(8) Valley fold the top triangle between the ears.

(9) The paper should now look like this.

(10) Turn the paper over. Valley fold the bottom corner.

(11) Valley fold the tip of the bottom triangle to create the cat's nose.

(12) You now have the cat's head.

MAKE THE BODY

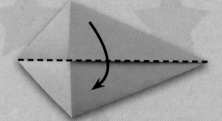

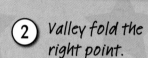

① Find out how to make a
kite base on page 6. Turn
it on its side, as shown.
Valley fold in half.

② Valley fold the
right point.

③ Valley fold the
right corner.

④ The paper should
now look like this.

⑤ Open up the folds you made
in steps 2 and 3.

⑥ Gently lift the right
corner and open it out.

open
out

Did You Know?

Cats use their whiskers to tell whether they can squeeze
through small openings. A cat's whiskers are always the
same width as its body.

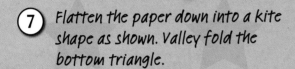

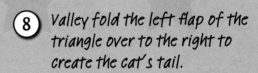

7) Flatten the paper down into a kite shape as shown. Valley fold the bottom triangle.

8) Valley fold the left flap of the triangle over to the right to create the cat's tail.

9) You now have the cat's body, as shown left.

PUT THE CAT TOGETHER

1) Balance the head on the top point of the cat's body.

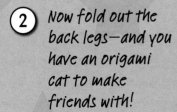

2) Now fold out the back legs—and you have an origami cat to make friends with!

Hamster

A hamster carries food in special pouches in its cheeks. When the pouches are full, the hamster's face can look enormous!

1 Start with a square of paper, colored side down with the point towards you. Valley fold it in half diagonally.

2 Open the paper and valley fold it in half diagonally the other way.

3 Turn the paper, so that the point is upwards, as shown. Valley fold the tip of the top flap.

4 Valley fold the tip of the flap underneath.

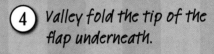

5 The paper should now look like this. Turn the paper over.

6 Valley fold the right corner to make a flap.

Did You Know?

Hamsters use their cheek pouches to carry food to their secret stores.

7 Do the same on the other side.

8 Valley fold the right flap.

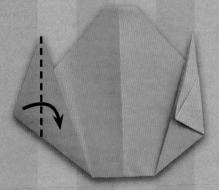

9 Do the same on the other side.

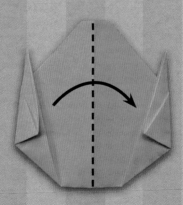

10 Valley fold along the center crease.

11 Turn the paper around like this. Valley fold the left corner.

12 Unfold, then make an inside reverse fold to create the tail.

Pull

13 Gently pull the ears up and out.

14 Now you have a cute origami hamster, looking for something to nibble!

Puppy

Puppies are cute and playful, but they can be very naughty before they are trained and housebroken! Here's a fun origami puppy, just for you!

Start with a kite base

1. Find out how to make a kite base on page 6. Turn it upside down. Turn the paper over.

2. Mountain fold it in half so that the top section goes behind the bottom section.

3. The paper should now look like this. Unfold.

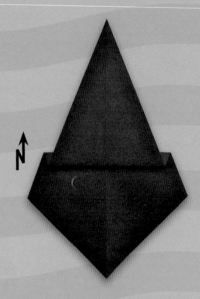

4. Make a valley fold just beneath the crease to make a step fold. Turn the paper over.

5 Valley fold the top point.

6 Valley fold the bottom point up to meet the tip of the top section.

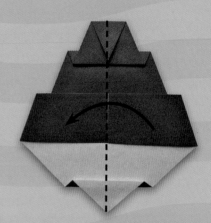

7 Valley fold the top section up and the bottom section down.

8 Fold the top tip down in a valley fold.

9 Valley fold the paper in half along the center crease from right to left.

Did You Know?

Puppies love to chew things. This is partly because they are teething, just like human babies!

Push

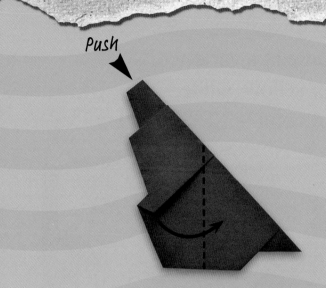

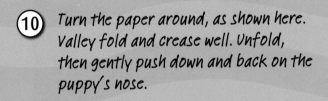

(10) Turn the paper around, as shown here. Valley fold and crease well. Unfold, then gently push down and back on the puppy's nose.

(11) As you push, the flaps pop backwards into place, revealing the puppy's white feet.

(12) Stand up your origami model, and you have a perfectly cute puppy playmate!

Goldfish

Although called goldfish, these fish come in a variety of different colors, including red, orange, yellow, white, black, and brown. Make yours a bright color!

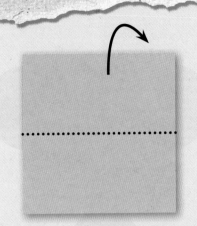
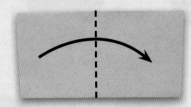

① Start with a square of paper, colored side down. Mountain fold it in half, taking the top section back behind the bottom section.

② Valley fold it in half from left to right.

③ The paper should now look like this.

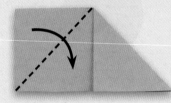
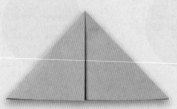

④ Open the paper out. Valley fold the right corner.

⑤ Do the same on the other side.

⑥ The paper should now look like this.

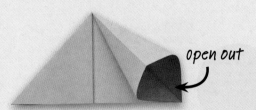
open out
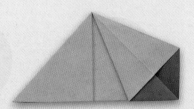
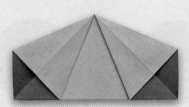

⑦ Gently open out the right corner.

⑧ Flatten the paper to make a kite shape, as shown.

⑨ Repeat steps 7 and 8 on the other side.

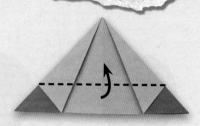

10 Turn the paper over. Valley fold the right corner.

11 Do the same on the other side.

12 Valley fold the upper flap.

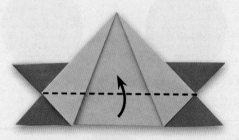

13 The paper should now look like this. Turn it over.

14 Valley fold the bottom section.

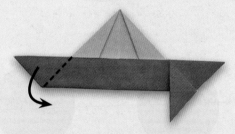

15 Valley fold the right upper flap.

16 Do the same on the other side.

Did You Know?

Some people say that goldfish have a 3-second memory. This is not really true! They can actually remember things for at least 3 months.

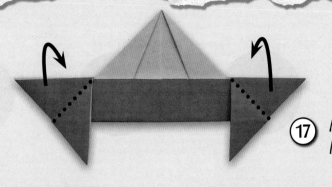

open up

(17) Mountain fold the right and left corners at the back.

(18) The paper should now look like this. Start to open the bottom out.

Push   Push

(19) Push the left and right sides together until they snap shut.

(20) Turn the model sideways, pull out the tail fins, and you have a fabulous origami goldfish!

Mouse

The mouse has an excellent sense of smell, and it investigates its surroundings with a long, pointy nose—just like this origami version!

Start with a fish base

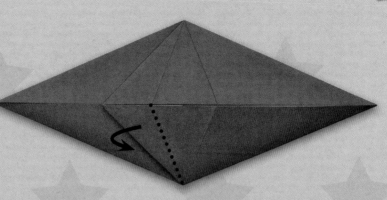

① Find out how to make a fish base on page 7. Turn it so that the flaps are pointing to the left. Mountain fold the bottom flap and tuck it under itself.

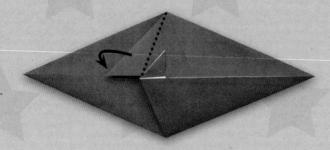

② Mountain fold the top flap and tuck it under the bottom flap.

③ Mountain fold the left point.

④ Mountain fold the top left corner.

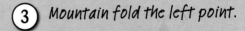

⑤ Do the same on the bottom.

6 Mountain fold in half, so that the top section folds down behind the bottom section.

7 Valley fold the front flap. Then do the same to the back flap to create the ears.

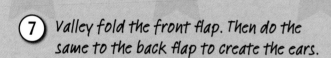

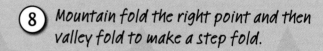

8 Mountain fold the right point and then valley fold to make a step fold.

Did You Know?

A mouse's teeth never stop growing. They must constantly gnaw on things to keep their teeth from getting too long!

(9) Unfold and do an inside reverse fold to make the tail point downwards, as shown. Then do a second inside reverse fold to tuck the tail back up.

(10) Mountain fold the right edge of the front flap of the tail to tuck it in and make it narrow. Do the same for the back flap.

Pull

(11) open out the ears and pull the tail down gently

(12) You now have an inquisitive origami mouse, complete with a pointy nose and tail!

Turtle

The turtle spends a lot of time in water. It has powerful flippers to help it swim. It also has a hard, rounded shell to protect it from predators.

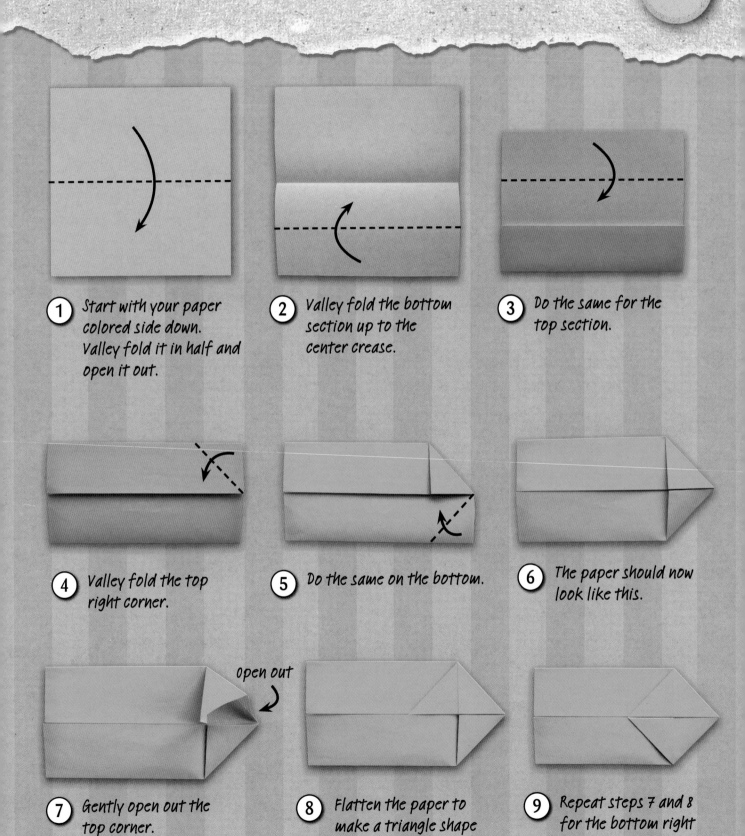

1. Start with your paper colored side down. Valley fold it in half and open it out.

2. Valley fold the bottom section up to the center crease.

3. Do the same for the top section.

4. Valley fold the top right corner.

5. Do the same on the bottom.

6. The paper should now look like this.

open out

7. Gently open out the top corner.

8. Flatten the paper to make a triangle shape as shown.

9. Repeat steps 7 and 8 for the bottom right corner.

Did You Know?

When female sea turtles are ready to lay their eggs, they return to the same beach where they hatched.

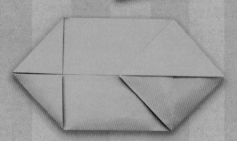

(10) Repeat steps 4 through 9 for the left corners.

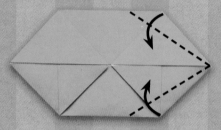

(11) Valley fold the top and bottom right corners.

(12) Repeat step 11 for the left corners.

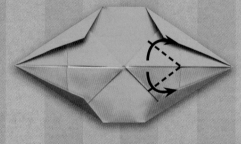

(13) Valley fold the flaps on the right to create the turtle's feet.

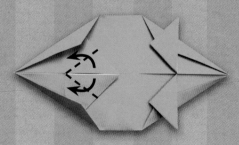

(14) Do the same on the other side.

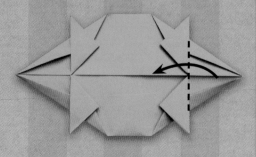

(15) Valley fold the right point into the body.

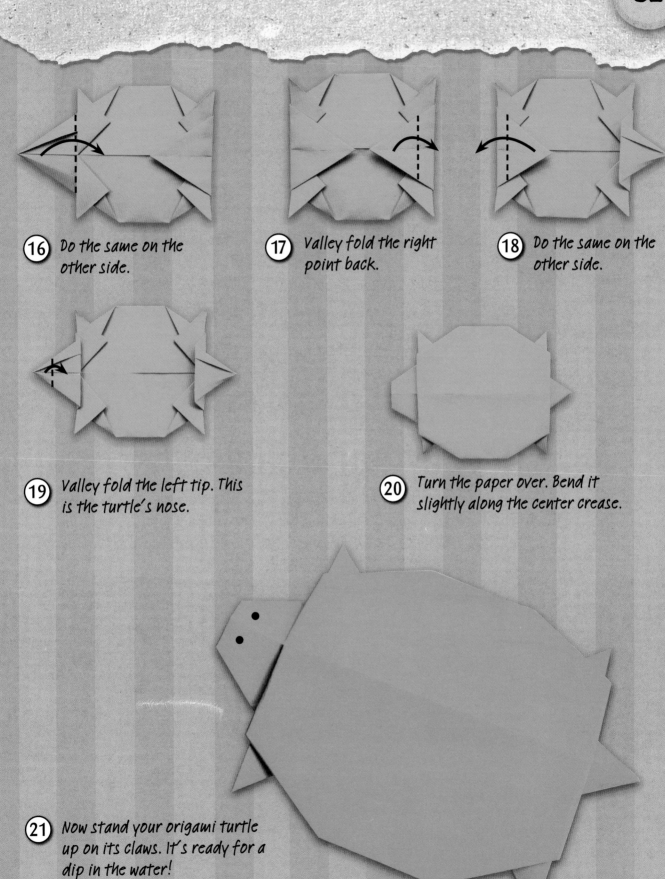

16 Do the same on the other side.

17 Valley fold the right point back.

18 Do the same on the other side.

19 Valley fold the left tip. This is the turtle's nose.

20 Turn the paper over. Bend it slightly along the center crease.

21 Now stand your origami turtle up on its claws. It's ready for a dip in the water!

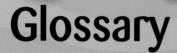

Glossary

base A simple, folded shape that is used as the starting point for many different origami projects.

crease A line in a piece of paper made by folding.

flipper A wide, flat limb, used by a sea creature to move through water.

gnaw To constantly bite something.

hatch To break out of an egg.

housebroken Trained to go to the bathroom in the right place (for example, in a litter box).

mountain fold An origami step where a piece of paper is folded so that the crease is pointing upwards, like a mountain.

pouch A body part shaped like a small bag.

predator An animal that hunts other animals.

step fold A mountain fold and valley fold next to each other.

teething Growing new teeth.

valley fold An origami step where a piece of paper is folded so that the crease is pointing downwards, like a valley.

Further Reading

Robinson, Nick. *Absolute Beginner's Origami.* New York: Potter Craft, 2006.

Robinson, Nick. *World's Best Origami.* New York: Alpha Books, 2010.

Van Sicklen, Margaret. *Origami on the Go: 40 Paper-Folding Projects for Kids Who Love to Travel.* New York: Workman Publishing Company, 2009.

Index